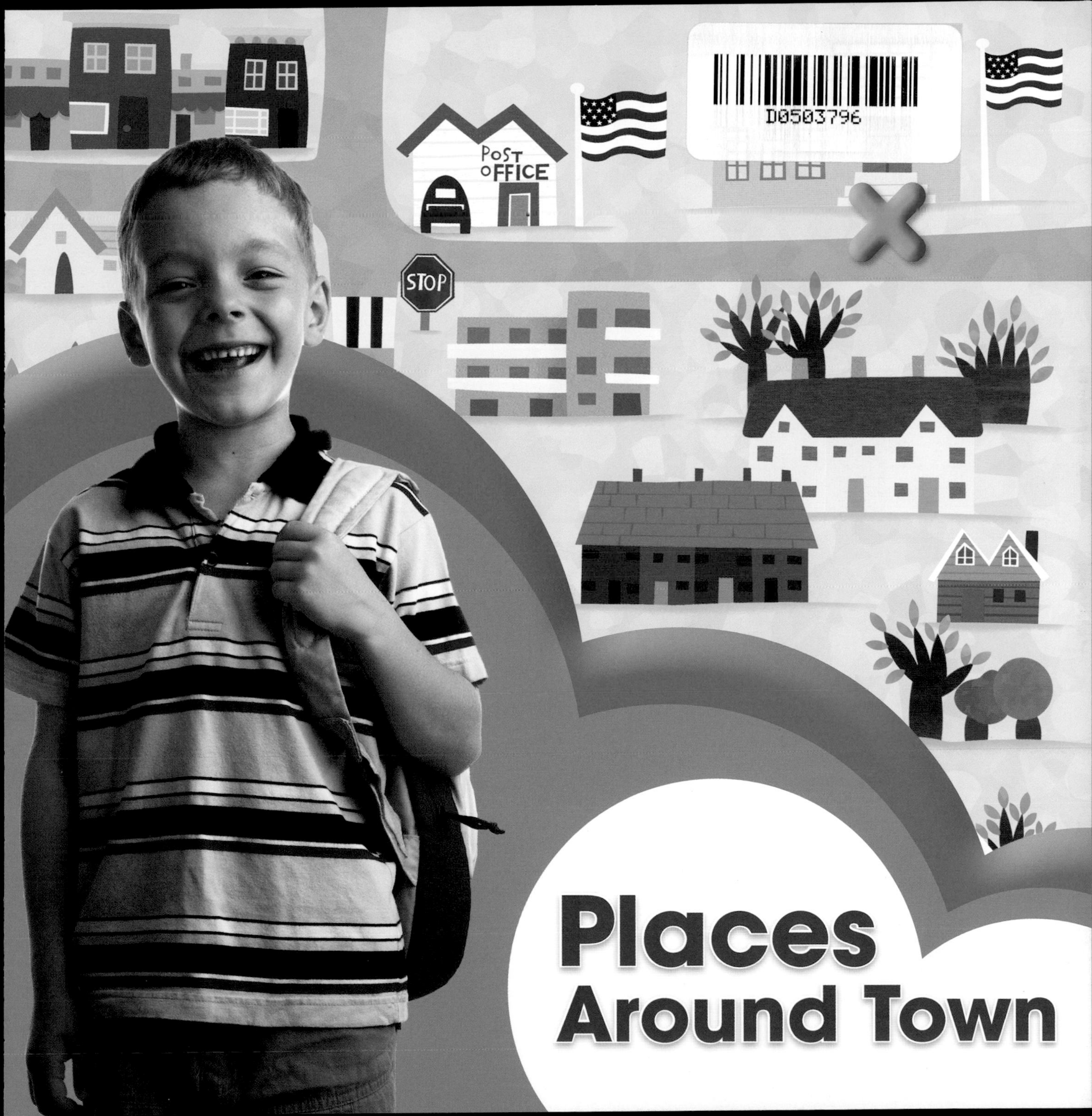

Places Around Town

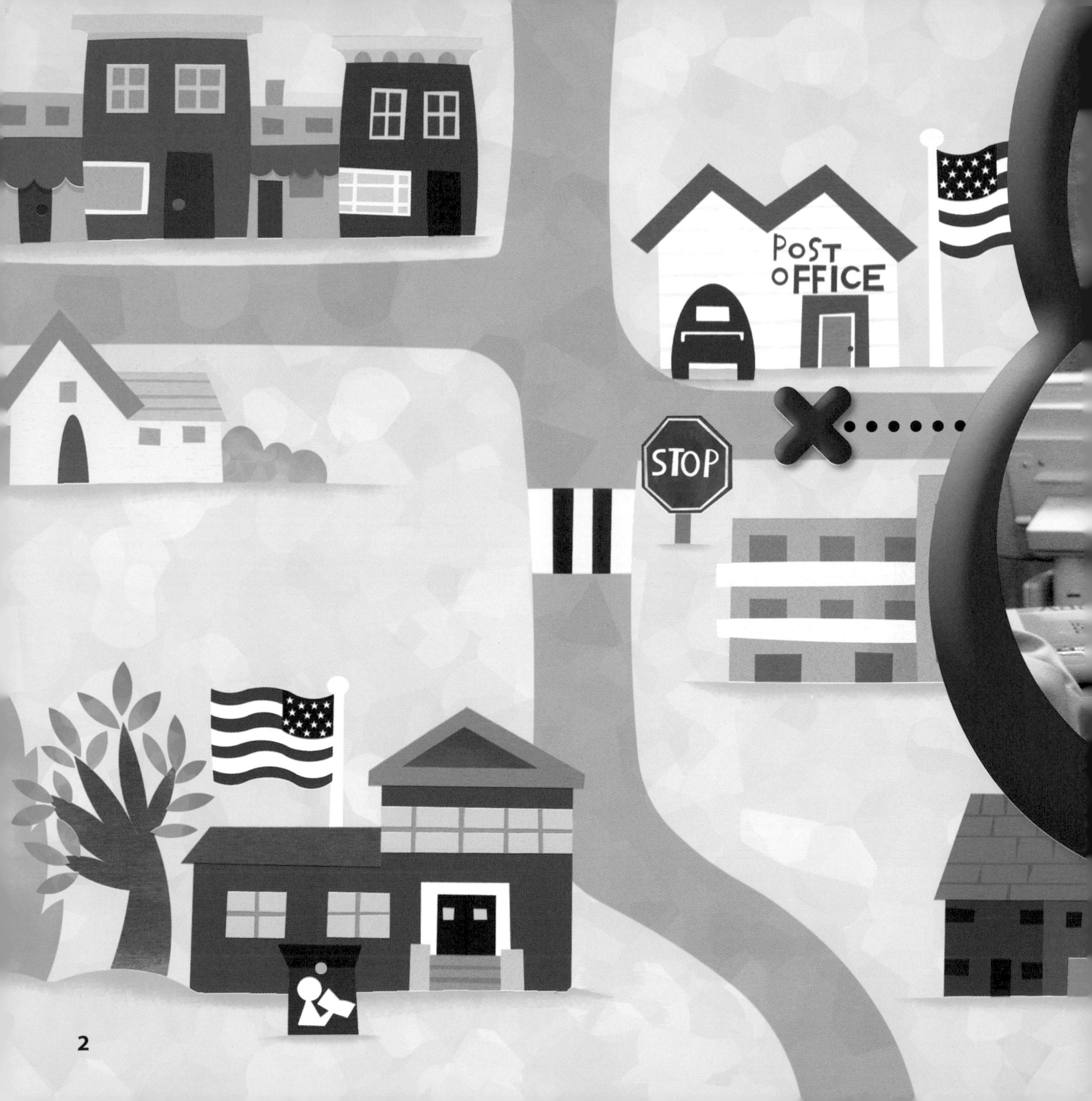
POST OFFICE
STOP

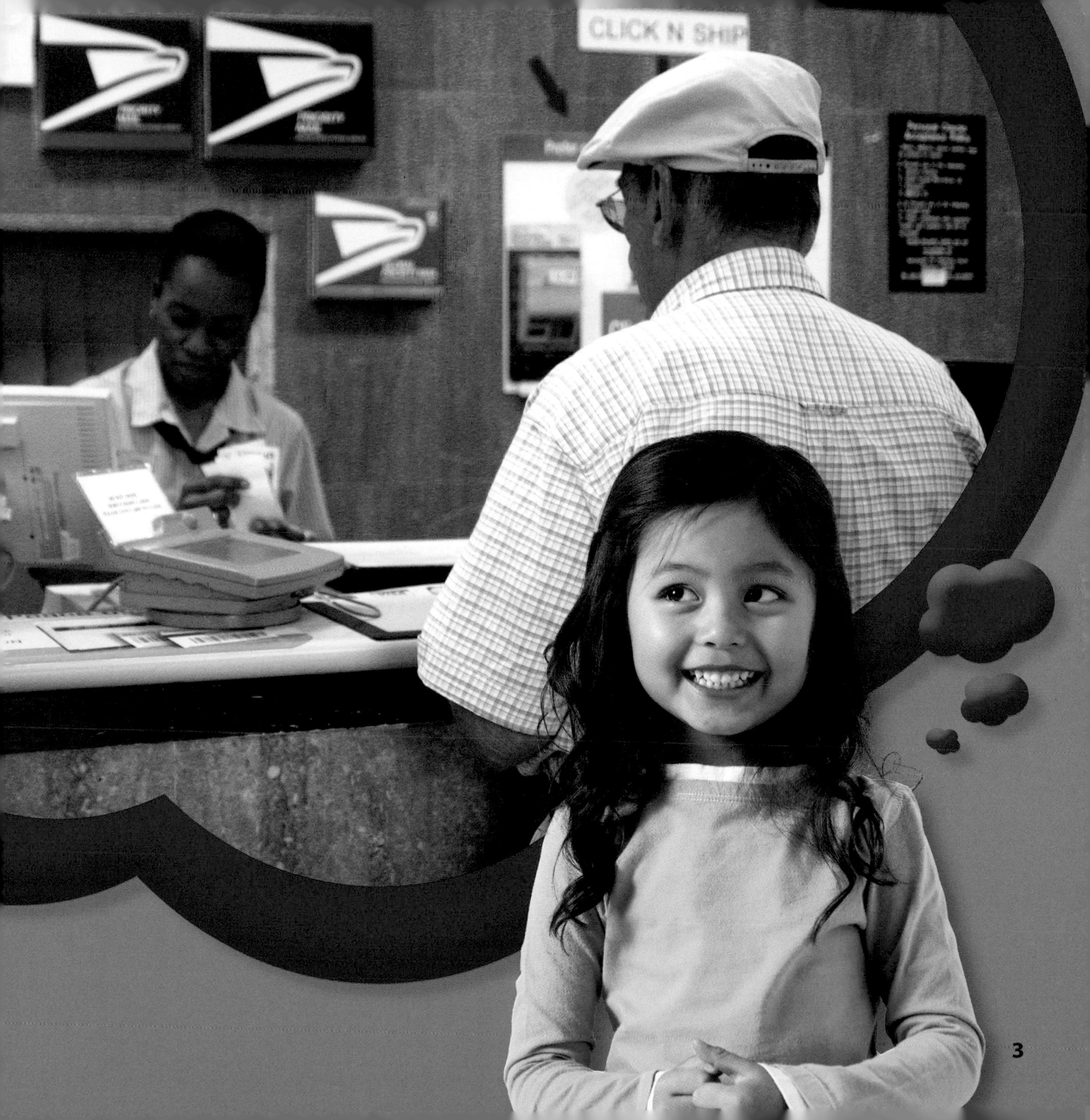
CLICK N SHIP

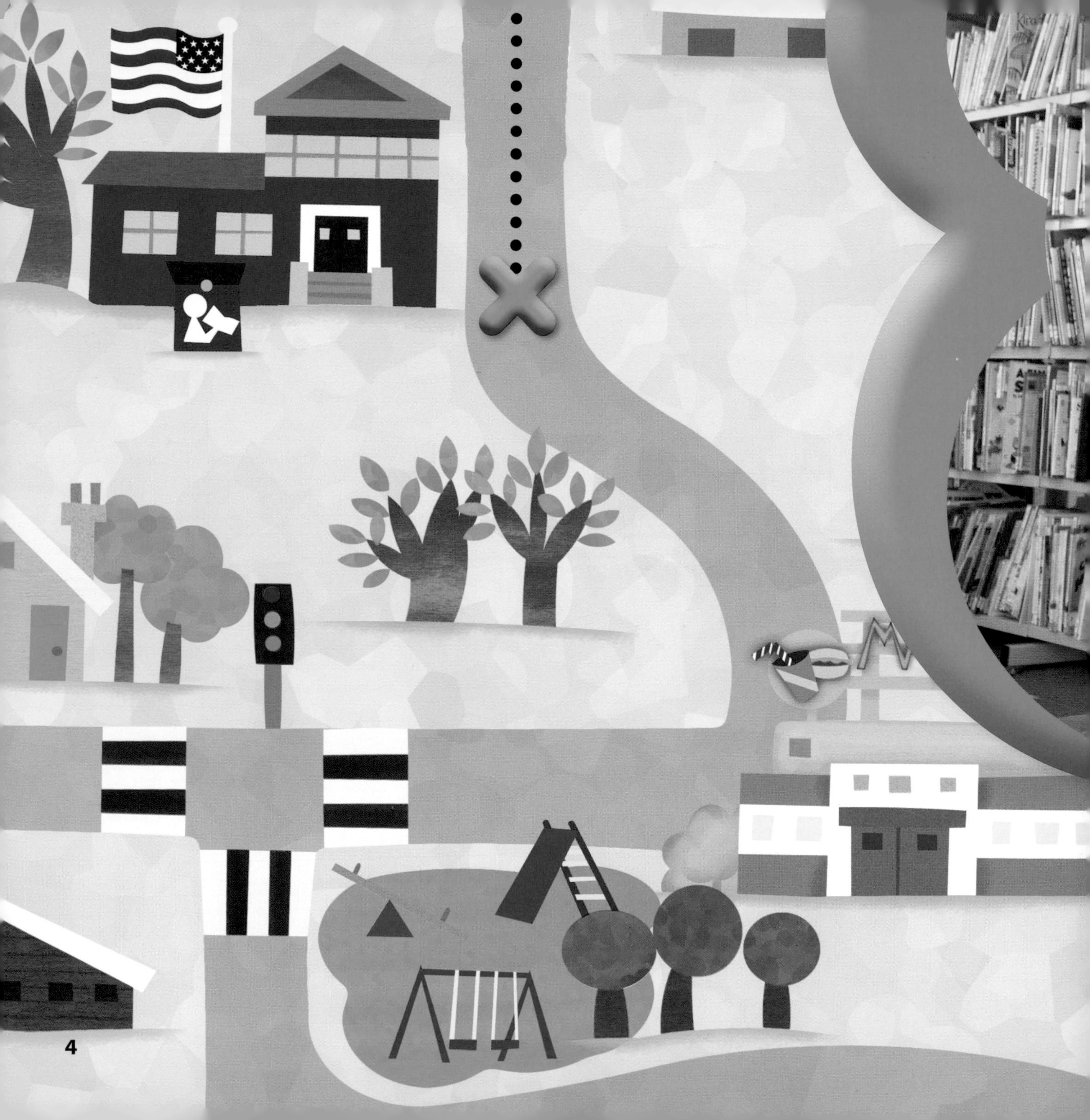

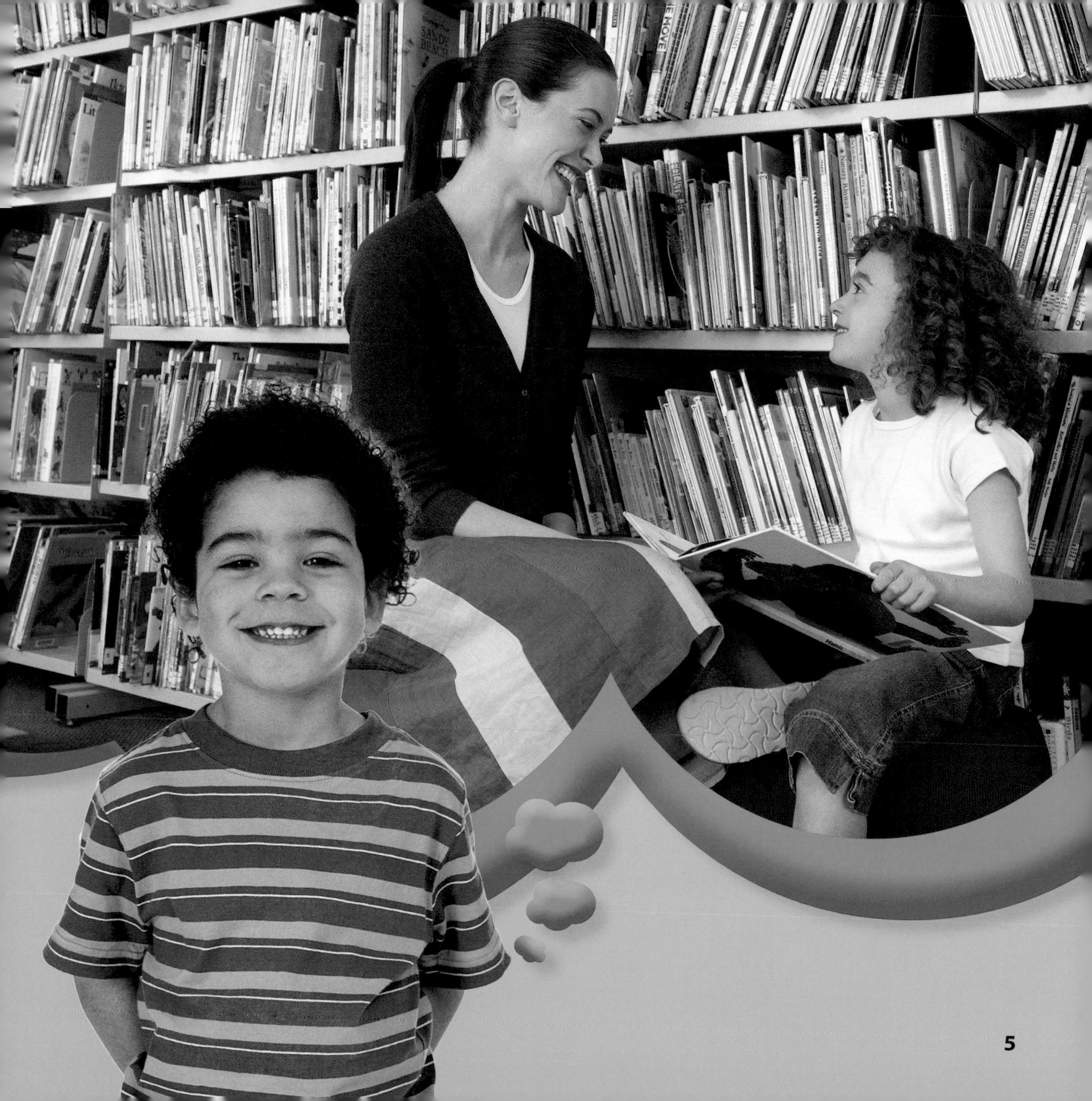

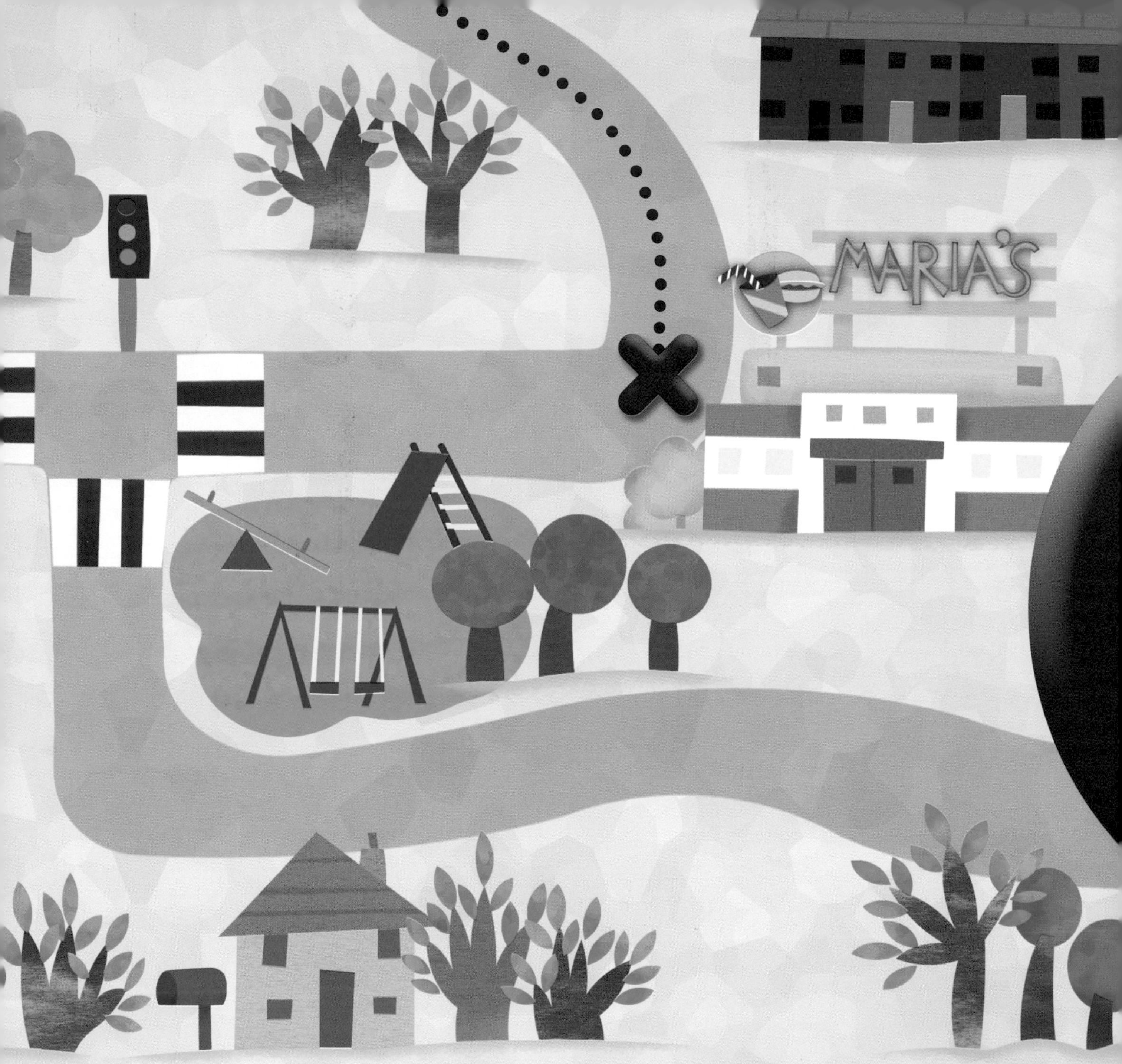
MARIA'S

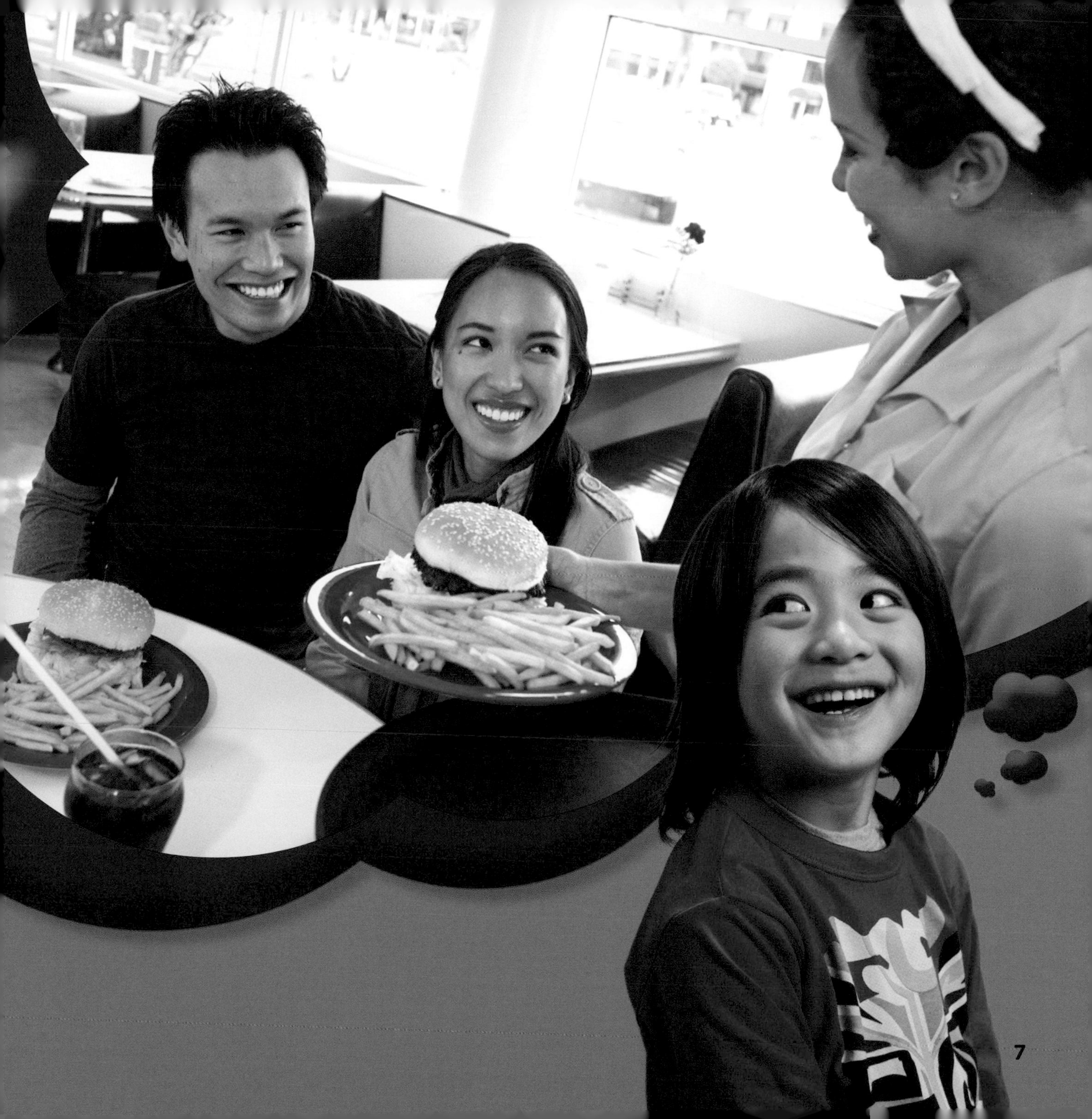

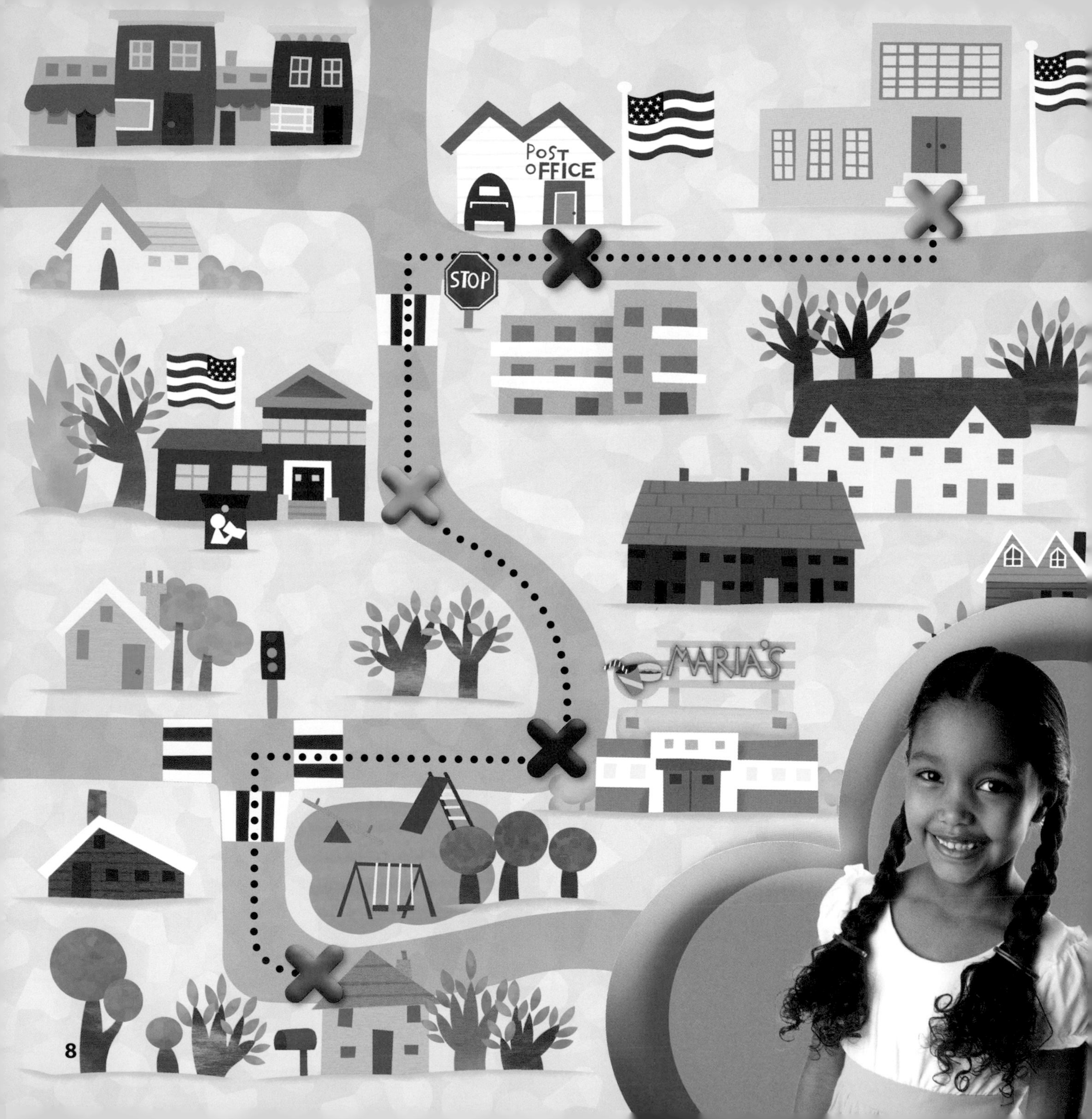
POST OFFICE
STOP
MARIA'S